LONGEVITY: WHAT CAN YOU DO TO LIVE LONGER ACCORDING TO MODERN SCIENCE?

Live Long And Expand Your Life Expectancy

By Sofie Bakken

LONGEVITY: WHAT CAN YOU DO TO LIVE LONGER ACCORDING TO MODERN SCIENCE?

Live Long And Expand Your Life Expectancy

By Sofie Bakken

LONGEVITY: WHAT CAN YOU DO TO LIVE LONGER ACCORDING TO MODERN SCIENCE?

Live Long And Expand Your Life Expectancy

BN Publishing

© 2020 by Sofie Bakken

ISBN: 978-3854627364

TABLE OF CONTENTS

DISCLAIMERS 6
INTRODUCTION 7
LIFESPAN AND MODERN SCIENCE 10
WAYS TO INCREASE YOUR LIFESPAN 23
    Eating healthy 24
    Exercise regularly 34
    Medical procedures 37
    Moderate sleep 43
    Education 44
    Stay busy 45
WHAT WORKS OTHER THAN SCIENTIFIC METHODS 47
CONCLUSION 54
REFERENCES 57
MORE BOOKS BY SOFIE BAKKEN 62
ABOUT SOFIE BAKKEN 64

DISCLAIMERS

Although the author has made every effort to ensure that the information in this book was correct at press time, the author does not assume and hereby disclaim any liability to any party for any loss, damage, or disruption caused by errors or omissions, whether such errors or omissions result from negligence, accident, or any other cause.

This book is not intended as a substitute for the medical advice of physicians. The reader should regularly consult a physician in matters relating to his/her health and particularly with respect to any symptoms that may require diagnosis or medical attention.

_____

INTRODUCTION

Middle age is a very tricky part of an individual's life. On one hand, you become fully mature and feel like you can tackle the challenges of life much better. On the other hand, you become anxious about what's coming ahead. You start imagining what old age might feel like and the reality of death becomes clearer than ever before.

But what if the 'middle-age' according to you is not actually middle age in the modern era? What we mean to say is, you might be getting worried sooner than you're supposed to. Thanks to modern science and technology, it is now possible to live longer than the previous generations.

Advances in science have had a significant impact on our daily lives. Whether it is the remote-controlled operation of electronics or staying virtually connected to people all over the world, the transformation has been extraordinary. Nobody could have imagined the current standard of living a few decades ago.

Moreover, the progress seems to continue unbound in the near future. Science is rapidly evolving and creating new opportunities continuously. It almost feels like a new world is emerging, full of previously unimaginable possibilities.

One such possibility is for human beings to live longer. Based on past data and research, experts are finding new and innovative ways to extend the human lifespan. They are continuously working to find a cure for deadly diseases and conditions related to old age.

Longevity is a relatively new concept for many people. It is still not as commonly discussed as it should be. In fact, the thought of doing something to increase lifespan does not occur to many until and unless they are diagnosed with a potentially life-threatening disease. But one should not wait till that point to start looking after small details that can go a long way in preserving sound health.

In science, the concept of longevity is better known as life extension. The term refers to all the medicinal and technological solutions for helping an individual spend more years alive than it was previously possible. The progress in this regard has been remarkable but going by the scientists' claims, we still have a long way to go.

The following text begins by linking the theory of life extension to modern science. After touching the various viewpoints of different scientists, it moves on to the practical steps that (according to science) increase your lifespan. Lastly, it discusses some not-so-scientific ways that may keep you healthy and ultimately help you live longer.

It is quite heartening to know that scientists are interested in causes that add value to the lives of the general public. Of course, there is some element of capitalism involved but the ultimate benefits of life extension measures are reaped by the old and unhealthy. So it is definitely good news for the upcoming generations.

LIFESPAN AND MODERN SCIENCE

A few things in life are predetermined by the universe. Some call it destiny/fate while others have elaborate scientific explanations for such happenings. Either way, one has to admit that certain aspects of life are beyond our control.

These include our physical appearance, our blood relations, the time of our death, etc. A few decades earlier, anyone would have just admitted that nothing can be done about any of these and lived his/her life believing that he/she is helpless. Now, it is one thing to submit to destiny, but it should never be the cause of despair for anybody.

Lately, something has changed about this approach to destiny. To put it simply, the emergence of modern science has given people the option to do something about the things that make them unhappy. It has given them a choice between helpless surrender and taking matters into their own hands.

"Choice" is an empowering word. It gives you the feeling of having complete control over the affairs. It is a satisfactory notion to be able to decide what you desire in life.

It is basic human nature to want to control the outcomes of all situations. Most of our anxieties stem from the feeling of uncertainty. We simply can't deal with not knowing what is going to happen in the future.

Needless to say, this goes against the nature of the universe. Our life is designed with a mix of certainties and mysteries. Wanting to know the mysteries will do us no good and only leave us frustrated.

Earlier in the text, we mentioned a few things that are beyond our control. But we also mentioned how science has paved the way for exceptions to be made. Let us try to understand these examples better by categorizing them separately.

Some matters belong to the fields of life that science has transformed completely. This is to the extent that it almost feels like they are within our control and not a stroke of destiny. Let's call such things what is 'doable' for modern science.

For example, in modern times your physical appearance is something that you can completely change using scientific methods. If you don't like your teeth, you can get braces to fix them. If you're unsatisfied with your weight and have no motivation to work out, you can use surgical procedures to tone your body. All in all, there's a solution to all your issues about physical appearance according to modern science.

Then there are the 'impossibles' even for modern science. This second category is not as flexible as the first one we discussed. There are things that even modern science is helpless about and this is what teaches us acceptance of things we can't change in life.

An example of this from the above text would be the blood relations that we're born with. Genetics is something that even modern science cannot change (and never will). Sure, you can have an adopted family and sever ties with your blood relatives, but you cannot stop being related to somebody. You can't do much other than accepting the reality, no matter how harsh it is.

Then comes the tricky part. The third category cannot be put as simply as what's 'doable' or 'impossible'. It is neither black nor white but falls in a grey area that signifies the mysterious element in our life.

For example, if our life is a painting canvas then this third category is where the different colors merge. In a gradient painting, when two shades blend into each other, there is a portion that identifies with neither (of the two) completely. It holds its own and leaves us mesmerized with its beauty.

To do complete justice to the nature of such things, let's name our third category 'uncertainties'. While these events are already prewritten in our fate, modern science can influence their occurrence. So we can't completely undo them but we can change them a little with the help of modern science.

One such uncertainty is the timing of an individual's death. Now before we discuss the perception of death according to the believers of destiny and the believers of modern science respectively, let us neutrally observe how the idea of death is perceived by the general public. If the mere mention of it made you a little uneasy, you know exactly what we're talking about. Whether it is a vulnerable teenager or a well-trained soldier on the battlefield, the certainty of death isn't easy to digest for most people. It instills a certain kind of fear which is unknown to many otherwise. It is a humbling thought and very unnerving for some people.

So much so that when the first signs of aging appear, we see people running to try all kinds of remedies to 'fix' themselves. This is mostly not because they dislike their appearance, but because it reminds them that they're inching closer to death. The idea of aging gracefully does nothing to prevent the overpowering fear that a dying person feels.

Alternatively, whenever a patient is advised to undergo surgery, his/her first question is what are his/her survival chances going to be. Even the people who feel like they have completely lost their will to live, want to turn back time when they feel like the end is near. The desire to stay alive may be hidden under layers and layers of despair, but it never completely vanishes.

We certainly didn't mean to scare you with all this gory discussion about death, but this fear of the same is exactly what we aim to address in the text that follows. When we say that death is one of the 'uncertainties' we do not mean to deny its occurrence. In fact, it is one of the biggest certainties that life as we know it will come to an end one day (unless you believe in immortality).

However, with modern science, you can add a few extra years to your life. While it doesn't put off death completely, it makes you feel less anxious about it. When you act on fear, you disempower it to a great extent.

The idea is to make you feel like you're in control even regarding the matters that are predetermined. This satisfaction makes you feel more content and naturally, more willing to stay healthy. It is of course in addition to the actual, effective ways in which modern science may increase your lifespan.

It is okay if the idea induces skepticism at first. But as we progress through this text, the role of modern science in deciding the duration of your life will be better explained. After all, you can never really judge the effectiveness of something without knowing enough about it.

Coming back to the point, modern science cannot accurately predict the duration of your life on this planet nor does it claim to multiply the years manifold. But with the latest research about the way a human body works, it is surely possible to add a few extra years to your life. How this can be achieved will be discussed in greater detail in the next chapter.

This is almost similar to the artificial method of condensation used in severe periods of drought. When it doesn't rain for a long time in a desert (or any other area), a system of precipitation is created artificially which showers light rain over the dry area. Nobody could have deemed this possible a few decades ago when science had not evolved as much as it has now.

This rain may not completely alleviate the issues caused by the drought. It doesn't also change the climate/weather conditions of the area. But it comes as a huge relief to all the organisms present in the area.

Basically, it is based on the principle of 'something is better than nothing'. It saves what it can and puts the living creatures out of their misery. You may choose to call this a miracle or a spectacular display of modern science.

If this wasn't something we experienced in our lifetime, we probably wouldn't even believe it. It might have even sounded a bit outrageous to suggest that science can do something that only nature is considered capable of. This is what we mean when we say modern science now almost stands parallel to the forces of nature.

The focus isn't on the predetermined factors, but instead on the things that you can do to influence those factors. Simple lifestyle changes supported by modern science can do wonders for you. Moreover, in extreme cases, there can be drastic measures to save a life if need be.

You may question whether there's any prior evidence of increasing one's lifespan through scientific methods. The answer is yes, this is already established through extensive research in recent years. But on a separate note, even if this wasn't the case just looking around yourself and seeing robots serving drinks to humans will tell you enough about what modern science has become capable of lately.

Speaking of its relation to longevity, in particular, there is no doubt that the human lifespan has been increased due to advances in science. However there seems to be a disagreement about things like the potential maximum life expectancy, how much of it has already been achieved, how much can it be extended further, etc. Let us have a closer look at the different views regarding these matters.

According to one school of thought, the maximum lifespan has already been achieved. In an article published in ScienceDaily in 2016, it was argued that we have already reached the maximum limit for a human's age. The article focused on a study carried out by scientists from Albert Einstein College of Medicine.

As per this research, a human being cannot (potentially) live more than 125 years. On average, the study puts the maximum lifespan at 115 years. Dr. Vijg and his team believed that this remarkable milestone was achieved in the 1990s (when a French woman died after achieving the age of 122 years).

The study also stated that the average life expectancy in the US had risen to 79 (from 47 in 1900). It also did not deny the upward trend in average life expectancy in many countries lately. So the argument is mainly regarding the maximum number of years a human can potentially live and not about the possibility of living longer for an average person.

Does this sound too confusing? Let's try to simplify the science. The scientists are still deliberating whether a human being can live beyond a certain age (125 in this example). They're not sure whether science can create ways to increase longevity beyond that.

But for the general public, it is sufficient to know that an average human now lives longer than ever before. The term 'life expectancy' refers to the average number of years that a person is expected to live. It has nothing to do with what maximum age has been achieved by somebody else in the world.

Another point raised by these scientists was that since the maximum lifespan has already been achieved (according to this particular research), the resources should now be directed towards increasing the healthspan. This means that a person should be able to spend more years in sound health. Ensuring longevity does not necessarily mean better health throughout the lifespan.

This is not something unique said by the team. There have been more claims suggesting that human beings may be living longer but they're also living a larger portion of their old age with certain illnesses. Before we discuss the authenticity of such claims, let's understand what are the issues that these theories aim to highlight.

Similar views about the healthspan were shared in another article published on Independent's website in the same year. The author provided data about people living longer but being ill for a greater duration as compared to the past (Griffin, 2016). According to the statistics shared in the article, the death rate from communicable diseases has declined sharply but people are just living longer with non-communicable diseases like heart conditions, diabetes, Alzheimer's, etc.

In simpler words, we're focusing on adding more years to the lifespan and not doing much to improve the quality of life in general. Deaths caused by non-communicable diseases have not fallen as much as those from communicable ones. While this is debatable, let's for the sake of argument believe that it is indeed true and see how it fits in with the theory of longevity. When a car is invented, only then can you realize and remove the minor faults within its engine. Without the invention, you cannot be talking about improvements. The focus remains that the new type of the car was invented and we have made progress as compared to the past.

Similarly, old-age issues cannot be worked on without achieving longevity first. Experiments and research are encouraging enough to let us try and remain healthier for a longer time. Besides, if you're alive albeit with a chronic condition, you're just one breakthrough away from being completely healthy.

So far, we have discussed only one kind of opinion about the maximum lifespan. There are other, completely different views regarding the same. For example, another article (also shared on ScienceDaily) as recent as January 2020, makes a phenomenal revelation.

This study carried out by Mount Desert Island Biological Laboratory claims that pathways that could extend lifespan by a whopping 500 percent have been identified. So if the longest lifespan currently averages around 100 years, this research means it could be stretched to around 400 to 500 years. We have to admit reading this momentarily makes you feel like you're a part of some sci-fi movie.

But realistically speaking, such groundbreaking research is what paves the way for future development. Like it is popularly said that if you aim for the moon you will at least land somewhere among the stars. Working on these pathways may enable human beings to live much longer than they currently do.

Another study says the human lifespan could soon cross 100 years (Franck, 2019). Remember this time we're not talking about a one-off example of someone crossing the century figure. Rather this is about the average age of the general public.

But this article adds a different dimension to the debate. It predicts that by 2025, the concept of longevity will be an industry in itself, that too worth $600 billion according to the experts at Bank of America. It is estimated that some of the bigwigs from the business sector plan to invest heavily in projects related to increasing a healthy human lifespan.

The prospects of any industry can be assessed more accurately when the business and commerce sector starts taking a keen interest in it. You can come up with the most brilliant idea but without the support of business heavyweights, it would be difficult to make it flourish. At least we can be sure that won't be the case with longevity.

To sum it up, the debate about technicalities only keeps getting messier. This is true for any kind of work in progress. Nothing can be said with finality about evolving concepts.

In fact, this is what keeps scientists interested and going. It motivates them to come up with modifications and make further progress. But to common people like us, it may seem a little complicated.

So, let us summarize the salient features of this whole debate for you. Science has made it possible to live longer. It is still evolving towards further increasing the limit of the maximum lifespan.

As an ordinary person, there are a few things that you can incorporate into your daily life to benefit from this development. The next chapter will focus on those specific practical steps. So, let this introductory chapter increase your knowledge but don't let it confuse you about longevity.

WAYS TO INCREASE YOUR LIFESPAN

Focusing on yourself is really important to attain an ideal and healthy lifespan. We often become so engrossed in our day to day affairs that we forget to take care of ourselves. Our busy work schedules, worries, and responsibilities consume us completely. The social obligations also add to this burdensome routine.

But we must remember that we can't be there for anybody else if we're not completely fit and healthy. Our professional and personal relationships will both suffer if we're physically or mentally stressed. We need to prioritize our health in order to live longer and not let our worries shorten our lifespan.

The concept of longevity is not complicated at all. It is about making slow and steady progress to improve your health. It requires you to work on your well-being so that you're better equipped to face the challenges of approaching old age. The sooner you start adopting these measures, the better are your chances of living longer.

So, let's get straight to the point. What simple yet effective things does modern science suggest in order to maintain better health for a longer period of time? We have answered this question in the text that follows.

Eating healthy

Reading the term 'eat healthily' may remind you of everything you have read on similar themes in the best. Let us first clarify that the diet recommended for different purposes has varying medicinal and scientific effects. For example 'eating healthy' for someone trying to lose weight has a completely different meaning as compared to somebody who is trying to gain some weight.

In childhood, you may have been part of a science experiment at school that involved white tulip flowers, water, and some ink. In this experiment, the flowers are placed in a vase/jar filled with water. Some ink is then poured into the vessel.

Students are asked to monitor the plant for a couple of days. To their surprise, in 24 to 48 hours, the petals of the flowers start turning the color of the ink in the vessel. The stems absorb the ink-filled water and the effects start showing on the surface of the flower.

The purpose of mentioning this experiment here is to highlight the importance of being careful about the food you eat. Consider the human body being the flower in the aforementioned example. Everything you consume will reflect in your mental and physical health, your appearance, and your emotional well-being.

Understandably, all these things also have an effect on the longevity of life. You may be wondering where does science come into play when we say something as vague as eating healthy food. It might sound quite repetitive to hear the same thing from your elders, medical experts, fitness enthusiasts and so many other people in general.

But modern science has changed the game by explaining the health benefits (or drawbacks) of certain foods we're already familiar with. It narrows down the exact scientific effect of the things we eat or drink for the relevant purpose. In this case, when we're talking about longevity, it cannot be a matter of trial and error. We need to be very sure about what we need to do and what not to do for the sake of a longer lifespan.

When we talk about eating healthy, we don't want images of leafy greens and tasteless meals to flash in your mind. In this section of the text, we shed light on some do's and don'ts of food intake in terms of life extension. The list isn't exhaustive, but it is comprehensive enough to get you started towards the ultimate goal of living longer.

Food that helps you live longer

This is a list of a few of the things that science believes would add a few extra years to your expected lifespan. You can consider these the 'do's' in terms of longevity. We have explained the relevant scientific effect of each item on the list to help you understand its link to lifespan better.

Turmeric
Turmeric has always been known for its healing and medicinal properties. In ancient times, if somebody suffered bruises or some kind of muscular/joint pain, a turmeric paste was applied for relief. Alternatively, it is mixed in warm milk and consumed for various health benefits in many parts of the world.

Now, science also links its consumption to a longer lifespan. Turmeric contains a bioactive compound known as curcumin. It is an antioxidant as well as an anti-inflammatory spice. (Petre, 2019)

According to one research, curcumin on its own may be insufficient in achieving the maximum health benefits. Increasing its bioavailability by combining it with components like piperine (found in black pepper) may work better (Hewlings & Kalman, 2017). When the maximum bioavailability is achieved, curcumin can work wonders for your immune system.

On the sidelines, turmeric is also effective in preventing diseases like cancer, Alzheimer's, arthritis, etc. It improves your metabolism and keeps cholesterol in control. As an antioxidant, it protects your vital organs from age-related damage and deterioration.

In Asia, turmeric is a part of almost every cooked meal. It is mostly used as a food color but the tradition has been passed on by the previous generations for greater health benefits. Even completely healthy people can use it as a preventive measure to increase lifespan.

The western part of the world seems to have woken up to the scientific benefits of turmeric rather recently. It has almost attained medicinal value and is sold in the form of capsules as well. Since it has rarely been reported for side effects and has innumerable health benefits, it is hard to deny its link to a longer life.

Nuts

Nuts are rich in fiber and proteins. They do contain fats but most of those are either monounsaturated or polyunsaturated fats. Moreover, there are several vitamins and minerals in nuts which are immensely helpful in boosting immunity.

Nuts are a great source of nutrition for all age groups. As far as longevity is concerned, it is now suggested that a handful of nuts should be consumed every day. An article published on Harvard's website hilariously (but also quite rightly) equates this to eating an apple a day to keep the doctor away. Citing research published in the New England Journal of Medicine, the article states that eating nuts reduces mortality from all kinds of diseases by 20% (Corliss, 2013). Nuts are great for your blood pressure and heart health. They reduce the 'bad' cholesterol called LDL and increase the 'good' cholesterol known as HDL.

Besides being good for your lifespan, nuts make for a delicious snack. There are so many recipes that you can try to ensure you never miss your daily dose of nuts. You can even eat them raw and feel like you've had a proper meal as nuts are quite filling due to their nutritious properties.

Garlic

Just like turmeric, garlic is also a part of every cooked meal in Asia. Lately, it seems like the countries relying on herbal and natural remedies have been doing more to increase their lifespan for decades as compared to the countries specializing in scientific and technological solutions. This is because now, modern science is also in agreement with many of the methods used in these ancient remedies.

Garlic works by relaxing the blood vessels and hence proves helpful against cardiovascular diseases (Matteo & Kelly, 2016). It is especially useful for people who are worried about high blood pressure. Garlic consumption improves the supply of oxygen to important organs of the body.

Luckily, garlic also enhances the taste of your food. So you won't feel like you're doing a burdensome chore for longevity. But if you still feel like you can't handle the taste or feel reluctant to add it to your food, it is also available in packaged form as capsules.

Coffee

Some people cannot start functioning properly until they've had their cup of coffee in the morning. It is not just out of habit but the drink actually refreshes and energizes the mind and body. But what you might not have known while sipping a warm, delicious cup of coffee on a cold winter morning is that it is not just soothing you on that particular day. It is also providing greater health benefits for the future. Studies revealed that coffee drinkers who consumed 4 to 5 cups of the beverage a day were less likely to die as compared to non-drinkers studied during the same period (Gunnars, 2019). Coffee is already adored for its various health benefits and utility in performing day to day functions. Now, coffee lovers have one more reason to drink it regularly.

However, excess consumption is also not recommended. The overdose of coffee is not as harmless as the aforementioned items on this list. A person should not drink more than 6 cups a day as it may result in negative effects on the health in the long term (such as high cholesterol).

Another caution in this regard is to avoid unfiltered (pressed) coffee. It has a compound called cafestol which is linked to increasing cholesterol over time. So, just to be extra safe, always opt for filtered coffee.

Apart from the few things that we have mentioned in the text above, some generally known foods can also help in keeping you healthy and increasing your lifespan. For example, fresh vegetables and fruits are always recommended for sound health. Anything that is free of preservatives is naturally good for your lifespan.

Foods that may shorten the lifespan

According to science, the following things are severely detrimental to your health. They put you at a greater risk of many diseases and hence shorten the duration of your life. Consider these the 'don'ts' of food intake if you're aiming to live a long and healthy life.

Tobacco and cigarettes

Many smokers think that cigarettes relieve stress. They feel like they're letting go of their worries one puff at a time. What they don't realize is that they're storing the worries in their lungs for the future. By the time they realize what they have done, the worries would have multiplied manifold, to the extent of completely destroying their lungs.

Smokers are expected to live 10 years lesser than nonsmokers. In an extensive survey published on CDC's website, smoking was termed the leading preventable cause of death in the United States. The data shared in the article also sheds light on the diseases (such as cardiovascular and respiratory conditions) caused by smoking.

Moreover, secondhand smokers also bear the brunt heavily. They also develop diseases like lung cancer and a heart condition and consequently have a low life expectancy. It is one thing to suffer from your own actions but the guilt of compromising the health of your loved ones should be enough to stop us from smoking. If you care about the longevity of not just your own life but also the people around you, smoking is a complete no-go area.

Red meat

The world is going vegan for all sorts of reasons. Some are concerned about animal cruelty while others avoid eating meat to maintain an ideal body weight. However, for health enthusiasts, meat (red meat in particular) is a bigger concern for a number of reasons.

Consumption of red meat has been linked to cardiovascular diseases, cancer, and diabetes (Ryding, 2019). The excessive content of iron present in red meat, along with some other compounds results in fatal heart disease and cancer. This theory has been backed by scientific evidence time and again from various parts of the world.

If you monitor the effects of red meat on your health closely, you may notice that (after eating it) you feel heavier and not as fresh as you normally do. Now that you also know it is bad for overall mortality, you should try to avoid it as much as possible. Of course, consuming it once in a while won't do any significant damage but regular consumption is something that needs to be minimized, if not eliminated completely.

Alcohol

Alcohol is an intoxicating drink. But so is the idea of living a long, healthy, and stress-free life. If you truly dive into this feeling, you won't have to temporarily intoxicate yourself at the cost of compromising your long-term health.

It is common knowledge that alcohol severely hampers your liver function. Moreover, it puts you at a greater risk of heart disease. Here's what science has to say about alcohol consumption.

Alcohol consumption could also lead to anxiety and depression, certain types of cancer, and dementia (Shmerling, 2018). Drinking too much in a short span of time may also result in alcohol poisoning. A short term effect is a lapse in judgment which may result in accidents or injuries.

According to experts, greater care is to be exercised about the quantity of alcohol consumption. As far as longevity is concerned, drinking 7 to 14 drinks per week can shorten lifespan by 6 months, 14 to 25 drinks could result in shortening the lifespan by 1 to 2 years, and consuming more than 25 drinks a week could reduce the lifespan by 4 to 5 years.

In the end, we must emphasize that discovering foods that lead to longevity is a secondary concern. First and foremost, one has to have the right intention to change the eating habits for greater sustainability. You're free to chalk out your own diet plan after carrying out adequate research. But you must remember that everything you choose to eat (or not eat) should be based on the principle of prioritizing your physical health.

Exercise regularly

In the previous section, we mentioned that the diet recommended for various purposes is entirely different. Similarly, the exercises required for different needs of the body also vary. But rest assured, exercise is definitely good for your health and lifespan.

Firstly, let's acknowledge the fact that any kind of physical activity is helpful. Whether it is a daily walk in the park or intensive workout at the gym, your body welcomes the improved blood circulation, the oxygen supply to various parts of the body, and the stress relief it provides to your mind and body. Just stretching your muscles casually also makes you feel so much better.

So again, the question is, where does science step in? Let's try to answer this question in two parts. Firstly, science explains the link between exercise and lifespan quite clearly. It provides results-based evidence that human intellect alone cannot provide.

For example, exercise reduces the level of inflammation in the body. The inflammatory markers (such as c-reactive protein) are reduced after exercise. This is probably why active people are less prone to chronic diseases because inflammation is the main cause of such illnesses.

In an experiment, people were monitored before and after a 20-minute walk/jog on the treadmill. There was a 5% reduction in cells that cause inflammation after the exercise. So it's not difficult to understand how regular exercise would contribute to keeping you healthy and adding a few extra years to your life.

There is a misconception that if you're overweight, light exercise won't help much until and unless you lose all the extra weight first. This is not entirely true. According to research, moderate exercise for about 75 minutes a week can increase the lifespan by 1.8 years.

Obese people can add 2.7 to 3.4 years to their lives by exercising for about 150 minutes a week. For people with normal body weight, exercising for the same duration can increase life expectancy by 4.7 years. In short, the more time you spend exercising, the greater would be your life expectancy.

The second contribution that science has had in longevity through exercising is by facilitating the modes of exercise. Today, if you cannot manage the time to visit a park or exercise for hours, there are technologically advanced machines to help you lose the same amount of weight within a few minutes. Some workplaces even have gyms installed within the premises.

The latest equipment is readily available to everybody. If you have the time you can join a gym or manage a quick workout at home as well. Some people even multitask by exercising at the same time as fulfilling their work duties.

If you're not used to exercising but want to start somewhere, anything like a brisk walk would increase your chances of living longer. Alternatively, if you already exercise regularly, push yourself to increase the duration or intensity to get better results. As long as you're staying active, you're effectively keeping many diseases at bay and ensuring a healthier life.

Medical procedures

This is where we get down to the specifics. Medicinal science has completely transformed during the past few decades. From artificial limbs to heart transplant, everything that seemed unimaginable in the past is now within the reach of science.

Since it would be difficult to talk about all the miraculous achievements of science in terms of increasing life expectancy in one go, we have divided this section of the text into 3 parts. In each part, we aim to discuss the relevant achievements briefly. While it would still not be enough to do justice to the phenomenal progress, it would provide some insight into the role that modern science has played in achieving longevity.

Diagnosis

With advanced technology, it is now possible to diagnose the root cause of your symptoms much more accurately. Sometimes a patient goes to the physician with minor symptoms like cough and an X-Ray or CT Scan reveals a bigger problem in the respiratory system. If it wasn't for all this progress modern science has made, the patient would have received inadequate treatment and died a premature death.

Some people have an irrational fear of proper diagnosis. If they feel like they might have a serious illness, they avoid getting a proper checkup. It seems like staying oblivious will make their problems vanish.

This fear proves counterproductive when it comes to increasing lifespan. The approach is equivalent to burying the head in the sand to avoid facing reality. An early diagnosis can be the key to living healthily for a longer duration.

It wouldn't be wrong to say that science has been a lifesaver in the area of prompt and accurate diagnosis. All over the world, health infrastructure is being improved so that people living in far off areas can be diagnosed and treated in a timely manner. If this can be matched with proper awareness about the lifesaving possibilities, the average lifespan can be further enhanced.

So what can you practically do to take advantage of the scientific progress in the field of diagnosis? An ideal way to stay aware of your physical health and any required treatment is to schedule regular checkups with your physician. Don't wait until you absolutely can't do without medical aid.

With age, the risk of developing certain chronic illnesses also increases. Instead of fearing the findings of a medical checkup, you can have the upper hand by nipping the problem in the bud. This way you will make the job much easier for yourself as well as the doctors and caregivers.

Advanced medicine

Imagine living in an era when a diabetic patient did not have easy access to insulin. Sounds a little extreme, doesn't it? To be very honest, our generation has been spoiled to some extent by the gains in the field of medicine. We don't realize the blessings that we have until we try to imagine a life without them.

Today a diabetic patient can be seen living a normal life with a daily dose of insulin. In the past, even survival was difficult for patients. This is the kind of impact modern science has had on medicines aimed at increasing life expectancy.

The development of vaccines for different ailments was a gamechanger for medical science. For example, most countries have successfully eradicated polio by getting the entire population vaccinated. What better time to realize the importance of a vaccine than today when the world is struggling to come up with a cure for COVID-19.

Consider the ancient times as the world facing several global pandemics all at once. We wouldn't be talking about longevity today if survival was not ensured by lifesaving drugs. There is continuous development in this regard which reflects in data available from various parts of the world.

The global life expectancy has increased exponentially especially after the 1918 influenza pandemic. The curve of life expectancy shows a steep ascent in the last 65 years (Desjardins, 2020). Before this, the average life expectancy was around 20 to 30 years with people dying due to easily curable diseases like diarrhea and pneumonia.

Although this chapter is about what you can do to increase your lifespan, we won't be careless enough to recommend taking medicines as you deem fit. We have already emphasized the importance of regular checkups and early diagnosis. However, if you're already prescribed routine medicines then you need to be very serious and never miss a dose. Reading about the dark and gloomy times of the pre-modern era should be an eyeopener for every one of us who is living with so many lifesaving medical facilities.

Surgical procedures

Let's assume someone had the misfortune of suffering a heart attack. After the emergency treatment, it is time to assess the damage done to the arteries or the heart tissue. This can be done through an angiogram or other high-resolution imaging tests.

Once the situation becomes clearer, the doctors decide what kind of surgery the patient needs accordingly. The choice, in this case, is between an angioplasty, valve replacement surgery, bypass, or heart transplant. The suitable procedure is decided precisely according to the patient's condition at that time.

So we have mentioned two kinds of lifespan increases in one example. The first is when the emergency treatment is provided and the second is one the functional life of the heart is increased through surgery. Then there are regular follow-ups to ensure the patient is responding well to the treatment.

Today, all this is like clockwork for medical experts. Even the general public is so used to hearing about such procedures that they don't seem like something out of the ordinary. But for a moment, try to understand the level of precision we have reached in providing the most relevant surgery to the patient.

This is just one example of the kind of lifesaving surgeries available today. You could have a problem with any other organ and medical science is equally capable of handling it. Even in the case of an accident, immediate surgical procedures can ensure your injuries don't prove to be fatal.

Now coming to the most relevant question, how can you make sure that you don't miss out on these available methods of longevity? Firstly, one needs to be fully aware of the options that medical science offers. You can do this by researching yourself or having a candid discussion with your doctor.

Secondly, you need to trust your physician's advice without any apprehension. Sometimes people get intimidated by the idea of surgery. You can always get a second opinion on your condition but until you address the deep-rooted reluctance for surgery, you will never be comfortable with the idea of undergoing it.

So, in case you require any kind of surgical procedure, you can find solace in the fact that medical science is advanced enough to provide it in a hassle-free manner. It won't cause any harm but actually, help you live longer. This is the sole reason all the progress was made in the first place.

Moderate sleep

You may have read articles about getting at least 7 hours of sleep a day to optimize your productivity. Getting adequate sleep is also essential in maintaining good health. Sleeping too little or too much can put your mind and body under too much stress or make it too lazy to perform.

As a result, your vital organs also start facing effects like fatigue and have trouble functioning properly. Along with your mental and physical health, this has a negative effect on your lifespan. Here's a brief summary of the link between sleep and life expectancy.

According to research, [sleeping less than 6 hours a day may shorten your life by 12%]. This may give you the idea to sleep extra and attain a longer lifespan. This is also not recommended by science.

The research also found that sleeping for nine or more hours could result in the shortening of lifespan by 30%. This was an extensive study based on results from 1,382,999 individuals. Most participants were over 60 years of age and monitored for 4 to 25 years to establish a link between the sleep pattern and mortality.

The crux of this whole research is to get 'moderate' sleep. You should not oversleep, neither deprive yourself of essential rest and wake up too soon. Ideally, 6 to 8 hours of sleep will keep you healthy and help you live longer.

Education

You may be surprised to see education mentioned in the list of ways that increase lifespan. Initially, we were also a little confused. But according to modern science, higher levels of education are linked to better mortality rates.

In an article shared on Time's website, it was revealed that a 2012 study by CDC's National Center for Health Statistics showed that people who had a bachelor's degree (or higher) had a greater life expectancy (Sifferlin, 2014). Highly educated people lived about 9 years longer than those who didn't study beyond high school. A health economist from RAND Corporation also backed this theory in the same article.

One aspect may be that better education leads to greater awareness about health matters. In the past, people were not capable of looking after their personal well-being as they did not know much about the way the human body functions. This has changed greatly because of modern technological facilities like the internet and virtual consultations.

The global literacy rate is now above 85% as compared to fairly low levels in the past. This clearly reflects the life expectancy as well. People are generally much more careful about their health.

Another aspect may be that the exercise that academic studies require from your brain may be good for your mental health. The activity provides some much needed mental stimulation. So, keep learning new skills to stay healthy and improve the chances of longevity.

Stay busy

Secretly, we all wish to leave all the monotonous daily chores behind and head to the mountains. Sometimes, work and personal obligations get so overwhelming that we feel like staying in bed all day long, doing nothing at all. Succumbing to this urge once in a while is understandable, but adopting this lazy approach generally in life is not a good idea.

You might be aware that pandas are known as lazy animals. But did you also know that they have an average life expectancy of about 20 to 30 years? If yes, have you ever tried to establish a link between these two facts?

What we mean to say is, just lazying around is not helpful in terms of longevity. The aforementioned article (on Time's website) also recommends remaining productive. Hard workers tend to remain healthier and live longer as well.

So, complete 'retirement' may also not be beneficial. Provide your body with the rest it requires but keep pushing your limits to do something that keeps you on your toes. Having something to do will make you less likely to give in to the woes of old age.

───────────────────

WHAT WORKS OTHER THAN SCIENTIFIC METHODS

In the previous chapter, we discussed purely scientific methods that have been proven to enhance longevity. But there are some general tips that we can pass on to each other that may help improve the quality of life. When you live better, you automatically increase your chances of having a longer life as well.

In this chapter, we plan to talk about the 'feel-good' factors that keep you healthy and may prove helpful in extending lifespan. Consider this more like a heart-to-heart when it comes to discussing the ways one can relieve mental and physical stress. As stress is often the main cause of most health issues, this would definitely help in remaining fit.

Of course, we do plan to share the scientific effects of these methods as well. But we do not claim that these tips are backed by science to surely increase life expectancy. Rather, (unlike the previous chapter) these are mere suggestions based on the experiences of most healthy, successful, and content people.

Mental health

Most of our adult life is spent worrying about work and personal obligations. Our responsibilities consume our daily routine completely. There is little time to do things that bring us joy and relaxation.

Some people have to work more than 12 hours a day to meet their financial needs. Some have a patient to take care of when they get back home. Whatever the case is, our day to day lives are just about juggling between different stressful tasks one after the other.

In the long term, this takes a toll on our mental health. Problems like anxiety and depression emerge because we have overlooked our mental and emotional wellbeing for way too long.

What should be done once you develop such conditions is purely for medical science to deal with. But a proactive approach would be to keep doing small things that don't let you reach that point. There's no guarantee that you won't face stressful situations, but if you're mentally at ease, there's a better chance of dealing with everything in a healthy manner.

Meditation

When you're stuck in an overcrowded room, you feel extremely suffocated. The moment you step out in the open, you breathe a sigh of relief. The fresh air is a welcome change for your mind and body.

Similarly, all the worries piled up in your brain make it feel suffocated. Having a few moments of peace every day can do wonders for your mental health. One must let go of all the thoughts and fears and let the mind relax for a bit.

There are a few ways to do this. Meditation does not require any hardcore training or technical method. It is simply about learning to calm your nerves by concentrating on a single object or thought.

If you have some basic knowledge of yoga, you would know that it requires you to regulate your breathing when you meditate. Similarly, many healers and psychological therapists try to alleviate your anxiety through deep breaths. Science has an explanation for why this helps.

There is a strong link between your breathing and the nervous system. Focused breathing can relax your mind and body and thus improve your health. Consider meditation as stepping out of a traffic rush (i.e the innumerable thoughts in your brain) to breathe a little on the roadside (i.e the few moments of deep concentration).

Spending some time in a quiet space, away from all the hustle and bustle refreshes your mind and improves your productivity. It enhances your mental and physical performance. Consequently, you feel happier and also tend to live longer.

Social life

There is a special reason for mentioning social life under the heading of mental health. Most people with depression or similar health issues feel extremely lonely. They either feel like they have nobody or that nobody understands them.

Before reaching that point (or to try to come back from it) we should surround ourselves with the right kind of people. The quality of the company you have matters a lot for your mental wellbeing. Someone may have a few friends and feel satisfied while somebody else's huge social circle may add little or no value to his/her life.

In order to prioritize your mental health, cut off all the toxic links from your life. Your growth depends on well-meaning friends, not the ones that cause stress and anxiety. Befriend people who encourage healthy discussions and advise you well at the time of need.

At the same time, don't get so occupied in your routine tasks that you forget socializing completely. Entertainment is also an important aspect of life. A hearty laugh with your friends can help you live longer, not the fear of what might happen at the next business meeting.

Music

Music has a profound effect on our bodies. Without much thought, our limbs start swaying when a soft tune is played. Our heartbeat follows the rhythm, accelerating when the beat is fast and slowing down when it is mellow.

You don't need science to tell you how experiencing music makes you feel. You can feel it in your soul and body. This kind of relaxation is extremely good for your long-term health.

Music is the go-to relaxation method for most people these days. This may be because it is easy to listen to music on the go whereas other hobbies or modes of relaxation require spare time and effort. Moreover, music makes your mood jovial and helps you through the day in a more productive manner.

So dedicating some time of your day to music might help you live longer. Some people even play light music to fall asleep more easily. It has a soothing effect on your mind and body.

Environment

Nature has a healing quality in itself. We're so used to living in concrete jungles that we're deprived of the nourishment it provides. The sun, fresh air, and natural environment are extremely good for your mind and body.

Demographics play a significant role in deciding the lifespan of a person. You may notice that people living in certain parts of the world live longer than the other. Various factors contribute to this.

For example, the cuisine of that particular area, the surroundings, the climate conditions, etc. You can't change the conditions that you have been growing up in. But you can try to adopt some healthier lifestyle choices from the areas known for longer lifespans.

The environment that most of us live in today is far from natural. The urban settlements do not cater to the needs of our mind and body like an untouched habitat. Imagine how far we've come from nature that we need an electronic air purifier in our homes today.

It would be too idealistic to hope that we can go back in time and preserve the good parts of nature. Clearly, we're heading towards a more man-made environment in the future. There would be more buildings and traffic and less greenery and birds.

But we can do something to connect to nature in our individual capacities. An occasional retreat to a scenic place helps a lot in refreshing your mind and body. Such trips make you more productive once you come back.

In the long run, looking after your mental and emotional health this way also leads to a longer lifespan. For instance, just having a beautiful plant at your workplace makes you feel much better. You can add some natural elements to these artificial surroundings to improve your chances of longevity.

CONCLUSION

You might remember the first thought that we shared at the beginning of this text. Middle age is indeed a tricky time for a number of reasons. But this is also true for any other process.

For example, if you're a school teacher, you tend to plan your lecture beforehand. You know how you're going to start the topic, you know how you'll wrap it up but what happens in between is beyond your control. Students might ask you unexpected questions, there may be some kind of disturbance or for whatever reason, the lesson may not go exactly as planned.

Alternatively, consider being part of a business meeting. The meeting starts off quite pleasantly, but it is in the middle of the discussion that boredom strikes. Or something might trigger your anxieties and all the 'what ifs' start creeping in.

We can list many more examples of a similar kind. The point is that you're bound to be shaken by challenges midway through any journey. At every new stage of life, there will be all kinds of trials and problems that you may not have faced earlier.

Staying calm and applying all the knowledge you have

accumulated over the years is the best that you can do in such situations. Ideally, during the youth period, one should spend as time as he/she possibly can accumulating knowledge, wisdom, and experience for the future. Even in the later years, it is a good idea to increase knowledge and equip yourself to face the challenges better. After all, the idea of learning something new should never seem 'too late'.

But all this knowledge would be of little use if it is not translated into practical steps and actions. You need to make sure that you direct all your energy into positive steps that improve and enhance your life. Understandably, this will also help you to remain stress-free and live longer.

This book is an attempt to highlight all such positive steps that you can take in order to minimize your worries about your expected lifespan. Like we mentioned earlier in the text, science is creating new opportunities for us. Now it is completely up to us whether we want to sit idle and worry about the future or take matters into our own hands and act on scientists' advice.

We hope that this text proves helpful in achieving its purpose. For the readers who were not familiar with the concept of longevity before, it will definitely set the right tone by explaining the concept adequately. If nothing else, following the healthy ways of living discussed throughout the text, you can definitely feel better about your life and also feel healthier mentally, physically, and emotionally.

———————————

REFERENCES

Can coffee help you live longer? (2012, September). Retrieved October 14, 2020, from https://www.health.harvard.edu/staying-healthy/can-coffee-help-you-live-longer

Corliss, J. (2013, November 21). Eating nuts linked to healthier, longer life. Retrieved October 13, 2020, from https://www.health.harvard.edu/blog/eating-nuts-linked-to-healthier-longer-life-201311206893

Desjardins, J. (2020, May 19). Global life expectancy has increased over the last 65 years - this animation shows it in just 13 seconds. Retrieved October 20, 2020, from https://www.weforum.org/agenda/2020/05/worlds-rise-life-expectancy-medicine-health/

Franck, T. (2019, May 09). Human lifespan could soon pass 100 years thanks to medical tech, says BofA. Retrieved

October 10, 2020, from https://www.cnbc.com/2019/05/08/techs-next-big-disruption-could-be-delaying-death.html

Griffin, A. (2016, October 07). Medical advances increase life expectancy but make people spend far more of their lives being ill. Retrieved October 09, 2020, from https://www.independent.co.uk/news/science/life-expectancy-average-healthy-lancet-diseases-when-will-i-die-a7349826.html

Gunnars, K. (2019, January 10). Coffee and Longevity: Do Coffee Drinkers Live Longer? Retrieved October 14, 2020, from https://www.healthline.com/nutrition/how-coffee-makes-you-live-longer

Hewlings, S. J., & Kalman, D. S. (2017, October 22). Curcumin: A Review of Its Effects on Human Health.

Retrieved October 13, 2020, from

https://www.ncbi.nlm.nih.gov/pmc/articles/PMC5664031/

Lifespan linked to sleep. (2010, May 5). Retrieved October 20, 2020, from https://www.nhs.uk/news/lifestyle-and-exercise/lifespan-linked-to-sleep/

Matteo, A. (2016, December 19). Garlic: The Key to a Long Life? (982234291 760644388 K. J. Kelly, Ed.). Retrieved October 13, 2020, from https://learningenglish.voanews.com/a/health-and-lifestyle-garlic-key-to-living-longer/3628672.html

Maximum human lifespan has already been reached. (2016, October 05). Retrieved October 09, 2020, from https://www.sciencedaily.com/releases/2016/10/161005132823.htm

Pathways that extend lifespan by 500 percent identified. (2020, January 08). Retrieved October 10, 2020, from https://www.sciencedaily.com/releases/2020/01/200108160338.htm

Petre, A. (2019, April 08). 13 Habits Linked to a Long Life (Backed by Science). Retrieved October 12, 2020, from https://www.healthline.com/nutrition/13-habits-linked-to-a-long-life

Ryding, S. (2019, November 21). Does Red Meat Shorten Lifespan? Retrieved October 15, 2020, from https://www.news-medical.net/health/Does-Red-Meat-Shorten-Lifespan.aspx

Shmerling, R. H. (2018, August 08). Sorting out the health effects of alcohol. Retrieved October 15, 2020, from https://www.health.harvard.edu/blog/sorting-out-the-health-effects-of-alcohol-2018080614427

Sifferlin, A. (2014, April 30). Science-Backed Secrets of Longevity. Retrieved October 20, 2020, from https://time.com/81573/how-to-live-longer/

Tobacco-Related Mortality. (2020, April 28). Retrieved October 14, 2020, from https://www.cdc.gov/tobacco/data_statistics/fact_sheets/health_effects/tobacco_related_mortality/index.htm

MORE BOOKS BY SOFIE BAKKEN

ABOUT SOFIE BAKKEN

Sofie is married with two children. She lives with her family in a European country. During the last years she got more and more interested in de-stressing her life and improving her life quality. She stumbled upon some European Nordic lifestyles that she examined thoroughly. Her studies also led her to the topic of longevity. She enjoys her family, nature as well as cooking and coloring.

www.ingramcontent.com/pod-product-compliance
Lightning Source LLC
LaVergne TN
LVHW040201080526
838202LV00042B/3263